Locked in

Story by Susan D. Price   **Illustrations by Brian Harrison**

Adam and his mom and dad
loved parakeets.
They had blue ones and yellow ones,
green ones and white ones.

The parakeets were in a big cage
in the backyard.

One day,

Dad put a lock on the cage door.

"This is a very good lock,"

he said to Adam.

"Now no one can open the cage

and take the parakeets away,"

said Adam.

The next day,

Dad went out to the birdcage.

He had some food for the parakeets.

He opened the door with the key,

and he went in.

Dad left the key in the lock

on the outside of the cage.

Then the wind blew the door shut.

Now Dad was locked **inside**,
and the key was on the **outside**.

"Oh, no!" he said.
"Adam is at school and Mom is out.
I'm stuck in here!"

Adam came home
on the school bus
and ran inside.

"Dad, I'm home!" he called.
But Dad was not in the house.

Adam ran outside to look for him.

"Dad!" he shouted.

"Where are you?"

Dad called out to Adam.

"Help!" he cried.

"I'm locked in the birdcage."

Adam ran over to the cage.
"You do look funny, Dad,"
said Adam.
He started to laugh
and so did Dad.

"Stop laughing and let me out,"
said Dad.

"You were right, Dad," said Adam.

"It is a **very** good lock."